Sunday at the Skin Launderette

i.m. Robert Simmonds

KATHRYN SIMMONDS

Sunday at the Skin Launderette

seren

Seren is the book imprint of
Poetry Wales Press Ltd.
57 Nolton Street, Bridgend, Wales, CF31 3AE
01656 663018
www.seren-books.com

First published February 2008
Reprinted August and December 2008

ISBN 978-1-85411-461-7

A CIP record for this title is available from the British Library

The publisher acknowledges the financial assistance of the Welsh Books Council

Printed in Bembo by Bell & Bain, Glasgow

Cover Art: Rachel Whiteread 'Secondhand' (2004)
Edition of 400. Stereolithograph of laser sintered white nylon. 11x10x16cm
© the Artist, courtesy Counter Editions.

Acknowledgements

Acknowledgements are due to the editors of the following publications in which some of these poems, or versions of them, first appeared: *Arvon/Daily Telegraph Anthology* 2002, Boomeranguk.com, *Exquisite Corpse, Magma, The North, NthPosition, Orbis, La Petite Zine, Limelight, P.N. Review, Poetry London, The Scotsman, The Shop.* 'The Boys in the Fish Shop' won second prize in the 2005 Ledbury Poetry Competition. 'Sunday at the Skin Launderette' won first prize in the Poetry London Competition 2006. 'My Darling, My Cliché' won first prize in the Wigtown Poetry Competition 2007.

Some of these poems appeared in the pamphlet *Snug* (Smith/Doorstop Books 2004), and the anthologies *Seren Selections* (Seren 2006) and *I am Twenty People!* (Enitharmon 2007).

Thanks to my family and friends, particularly Lisa Smith, Meryl Pugh, Anna Ziegler, James Manlow, Stephen Keyworth and Mimi Khalvati. Thanks are also due to the Jerwood Foundation and The Society of Authors.

Contents

The World Won't Miss You for a While

Lie down with me you hillwalkers and rest.
Untie your boots and separate your toes,
ignore the compass wavering north/north-west.

Quit trailing through the overcrowded streets
with tinkling bells, you child of Hare Krishna.
Hush. Unfurl your saffron robes. How sweet

the grass. And you, photographer of wars,
lie down and cap your lens. Ambassador,
take off your dancing shoes. There are no laws

by which you must abide oh blushing boy
with Stanley knife, no county magistrates
are waiting here to dress you down: employ

yourself with cutting up these wild flowers
as you like. Sous chef with baby guinea fowl
to stuff, surveillance officer with hours

to fill, and anorexic weighing up a meal,
lie down. Girl riding to an interview,
turn back before they force you to reveal

your hidey holes. Apprentice pharmacist,
leave carousels of second generation
happy pills. The long term sad. And journalist

with dreams, forget the man from Lancashire
who lost his tongue, the youth who found it,
kept it quivering in a matchbox for a year.

The Boys in the Fish Shop

This one winds a string of plastic parsley
around the rainbow trout,
punnets of squat lobster and marinated anchovy,
the dish of jellied eels
in which a spoon stands erect.
He's young, eighteen perhaps,
with acne like the mottled skin of some pink fish,
and there's gold in his ear, the hoop of a lure.
The others aren't much older,
bantering in the back room,
that den of stinking mysteries
where boxes are carried.

The fish lie around all day,
washed-up movie stars
stunned on their beds of crushed ice.
The boys take turns to stare
through the wide glass window,
hands on hips, an elbow on a broom,
lost for a moment in warm waters until
Yes darling, what can I get you?
and their knives return to the task,
scraping scales in a sequin shower,
splitting parcels of scarlet and manganese.
Their fingers know a pound by guesswork,
how to unpeel smoked salmon,
lay it fine as lace on cellophane.
A girl walks past, hair streaming,
and the boy looks up,
still gripping his knife, lips parting in a slack O.

Talking to Yourself

It starts with sounds of which you're unaware:
the window, opening, gives a rusting sigh,
saying something, although there's no one there.

The bath brims over while you ask the air
what's the point? The air makes no reply.
It's used to sounds of which you're unaware.

Children see you chattering and stare,
and mothers with their trolleys wonder why
you're whispering, although there's no one there,

just artichokes, an avocado pear –
they cannot tell you how to live and die,
they're lipless, though they may still be aware.

Inside the church the shadows lisp a prayer,
and votive candles clamber to the sky,
insisting something, although there's no one there:

the priest has gone, the altar's been stripped bare.
You've never prayed, but now you kneel and try:

it starts with sounds of which you're unaware,
saying something, although there's no one there.

The Dead are Dead

And still we long to break their silences, just as we did
when they were alive (*a penny for your thoughts*).

Did I say they? I'm talking about you of course,
about the way I thought I'd spin and spot you

slipping through the kitchen door with one last word
or squint and see your pale double in the mirror

throwing out a parting gag. But not
a whisper or a wobble. My Private Eye smokes

under streetlamps while I sleep, ready to return
another snap, a fragment of your speech. The dead

are dead, of course, so why is it I leave a tape-
recorder running in the dark to wake and play

back sibilance, which might be someone straining
to make sense? Why do I find I'm daydreaming

of mediums with microphones, a hall of strangers trooping
in with restless ghosts beneath their overcoats as if

they'd swallowed up their loved ones whole.
"Does the initial J mean anything to you? She tells you

to be careful of your back. She's happy and she sends
you love." Why do I want a postcard scribbled from

'the other side' *Wish you were here*. Full of platitudes
and sound advice. Are all ghosts sentimentalists? Are you?

Leftovers

Lit like a tabernacle, the fridge
does not contain a miracle
but only bits of bits in bowls.

The cat meows; the soft drum
of her belly beats for rollmop,
milk slops, bacon rind.

She'll have to wait: life is full
of hanging around, I tell her.
(Mung beans? Ratatouille? Skate?)

The bachelor across the way
falls on his knees, reaches in the dark
for jars, while next door

lovers offer one another hearts
and cauliflowers, or pasta shells
the shape of babies' ears.

Upstairs, someone whose post
I once received weighs up
his appetite for take-away, walks

a Yellow Pages round and round
the hard wood floor.
In time, a scrap of moon appears.

I haven't seen the muffin man
for years, or met a pieman
going to a fair, I've only stood here

talking to the Tupperware,
the dining table laid with light,
old receipts and unpaid bills,

working out a way of using up
these failing greens, a recipe
for half a weightless aubergine.

Reasons to be Cheerful

Cross-stitching in the fingers of old women
who have loved, and council flats in cherry light
which knows no class distinctions.

Patients gulping jelly in the hospitals
and varnished floorboards splitting water
into glassy baubles. Bumblebees

at work or profligate, and fountains
in the middle of the city where the hearts
of artichokes are being eaten in a snack.

The language of the women on the train,
the way it made them sift the air
with power to divine the dreams of mice,

to say all that's impossible for diplomats.
The table cloths at Ronny Scott's;
the orange sunflowers on your bed;

seahorses living their exquisite lives in miniature,
and Stevie Wonder being born.
The fact that someone must have improvised

before the tambourine; that *over easy*
is a fried egg giving up
its golden yolk without distress;

that bowling balls are solid molecules of hope,
and Margot Fonteyn danced at fifty-six
as Juliette, long-haired and loved by Nureyev.

Seahorses

Dawn: like eighteenth century
coquettes they court each other
crowned with coronets, blushing
pale yellow or vermillion,
linking their prehensile tails;
floating flirts, pot-
bellied dancers

defecating in a swirl,
riding through the themes of eel-
grasses, mangroves, water weeds;
dainty freaks, slowest swimmers
of the sea. Camouflage is
all they have, their
charm to fend off

Chinese chefs who pluck them from
their beds and drop them into
glassy soups, fan their tender
bodies over canapés.
Shamans powder them to cure
impotency
or a wheeze, and

trinket peddlers pinch them too,
dry them in the sun until
they're fossilised, set them in
the man-made amber of a
paperweight, or string them by
the seraphs of
their necks like slight

Lolitas. Miraculous
medals. Meanwhile, we shadow
them, peering from our darkness
at their curlicues of light
like aquarium voyeurs
biding our time.
Jewel thieves. Hunters.

Before a Make-up Bag

O the wonders he has done!
The flowers of the field
must pale and die,
the mountains pass away
and yet these stems of smelted gold,
these *Ice-cream Storms,*
these *Coffee Lusts* will last.

Praise him for the angel face
and second chance of it,
the *would you care to dance*
of it. Rejoice in brushes
soft as vixen tail, blues
mirroring the wings
of hummingbirds, pinks
like sunsets on Montego Bay.

Sing out your songs
in boudoirs, planes and strange hotels;
praise the great creator
frowning in his lab coat,
lifting test tubes to the light,
(*Chantilly Lace, Eternal Flame*)
finding ways of making good

the faulty work of God.
Thank him in his bounty
for the cupid's bow
and Lady Muck of it, the
In thee alone I trust of it,
the *Till death us do part* of it,
when even then I pray
I will be caked in it
and glowing underground.

The Men I Wish I'd Kissed

Adrian, two rows in front as we sang
Yellow Bird, way up in Banana tree.
I sang for him,
his yellow hair.
His perfect pale ears.

Prematurely stubbled Mark
who never spoke to me, but ruled
the pack of fourth year girls –
his silver Zippo
seeking their Silk Cuts –
while I stared out at other boys
on other buses, school ties loose
as snapped lassos.

Dan, the eldest brother of my next-best friend,
all monosyllables and eyelashes,
exiting from his dark room
where Blondie offered up
her pop star breasts.

A man from Padua who asked if he might
kiss me at a party once, though
I declined. Prim fool:
I didn't know then kisses are just foreign fruits
that you should always try.

Alan Alda in his *M*A*S*H* years,
gangly and sweet and able
to tell jokes while saving lives.

Tan-chested Dustin Hoffman in *The Graduate*
for whom I wouldn't mind the stoop.

And English men, not movie stars
but ordinary English men –
the one I trailed this hot spring afternoon,
who peeled off his t-shirt
clean as avocado from the skin
and walked half bare
before the gently frothing cherry trees.

Moonlighting

Last night you had a walk-on
as a Spanish waiter
in my dream.
How tanned you were
and how surprised I was to see you
in your startling white tunic,
servile and a little sad.

Women Dancing

They are dancing
to songs from years ago,
songs about refusing to give up,
let go, give in.
Love is their baseline.

A village hall, not enough men:
those who *have* come
preoccupied with banter,
noticing the dancers
absently through pint glasses –

royals at a pageant
put on for their benefit.
But the women go on dancing,
those who can,
those who cannot;

see how they fill uncertainty
with their best guesswork
when the rhythm changes,
see that one in red,
flying herself like a flag.

The buffet is poor,
vol-au-vents filled with cottage cheese,
quiche cut into eighths.
But a new year is beginning,
the records are cued up

and the women still have their bodies,
that same anticipation
for the next song,
which might be the one they have chosen,
which might be the one they love.

Precautionary Poem

In order to keep it warm,
I have bought my heart
a tiny duffel coat,
fur lined and toggled
with a hood to keep the hail away.

Because it has no ability
to absorb even simple information,
for example, Cause and Effect,
I have bought my heart
a Dunce's hat
to shame it for its foolishness.

And because it is frequently restless,
I have bought my heart
a set of flannelette pyjamas
so it will sleep soundly all night
and not wake early,
hopeful and profoundly tired.

My Darling, My Cliché

Don't start what you can't diminish.
A bird in the hand is worth nothing if it lies
stock still and won't sing. You can lead
a horse to water but you can't make it recite the rosary.
If I said you had a beautiful body would you.
This is our bed you have made for yourself.
Beware of old lovers bearing gifts. A rolling stone
gathers much loss. If you can't say something nice
say something with gall (many a true word
was said in a vest at three a.m. on a Wednesday night).
Why not begin afresh, put the past beside us,
forgive and beget? What the heart
hasn't seen the eye doesn't grieve for.
Please. It's not over till the. Oh.

Five Solutions

1.
Answer ads to see the room.
Sip tea with strangers, question them about the council tax.
Answer other ads; go to see a mountain bike, a baby's crib, a set of velour-covered chairs.

2.
Pretend you have no home.
Sit on the street and chat to kindly passers by.
Accept a cup of tea.
Sing *The Man who Broke the Bank at Monte Carlo*
watching all the legs go by,
deep inside your sleeping bag, at last outside yourself.

3.
Go to church.
Raise your voice beside the Presbyterians or Catholics,
sing out *Jerusalem* and think of school.
Sit when the priest invites you to.
Shake his hand (so warm). Jump at the chance of tea.

4.
Find a book shop.
When you're sick of silent browsing, stuff
a hardback copy of Samuel Pepys' *Diary* inside your shirt.
Get caught.
Spend an hour with the manager. Later
meet the police (more tea).
While away a pleasant afternoon with statements etc.
Make a date to see the magistrate.

5.
When there are no books, or mountain bikes or churches, simply
step out for a pint of milk.
Enjoy the change, cool in your hand, the smile and thanks.
Get home and put the kettle on.
Opening the fridge, discover it is white inside. A wall
of milk. A wall so white it seems as if there's nothing there.

Whittington's Mistake

He'd heard the streets were paved with God
and so he made his way
across the fields and country roads
one shining April day

towards the new metropolis
where riches might be found,
where men might see the face of God
by looking to the ground.

His cat chased after city mice
she caught them in her jaws,
while he sought out the maker of
their limp and perfect paws.

He strained the fountains faithfully
for some celestial sight,
only finding sovereign pieces
solid in his bite –

but no amount of gold could buy
the thing he wanted most,
a glimpse of the Almighty – Father
Son and Holy Ghost.

Summer came and autumn came,
and winter's white amen:
too tired to kneel, he called his cat
and they turned home again.

Transfiguration

Let's call you Dave. Let's get you out of sandals,
tie the hair back, better, shave it off.
Let's put you in a pair of low-slung jeans. Smile
without the suffering, be Beckham-like;
leave the lepers and the withered hands,
the herds of suicidal swine; the water into wine.
Tax collectors. Fishermen. Let's have you strolling
through the Kings Road on a Saturday calling
all the wounded out of Boots and Waterstones.
Command them to switch off their mobile phones.
Tell them stories that will save them, Dave,
tell them how you healed the crippled of their debt,
led the lonely from their stacks of DVDs,
the desperate from another night of alcopops
and nightclub brawls. Show them how you feed five thousand
with a single Prêt-a-Manger tuna mayonnaise.
Take them to the Serpentine and row them out
(they're wearing their expensive shoes, they're scared)
offer them your hand until they're balanced, backlit,
stained glass angels on the water's quivering lip.

At 8:53 p.m. my Television Breaks

With two hands on its shoulders
I try rocking it to sense,
like a priest conducting an exorcism

gone badly wrong,
or a woman in a soap opera, desperate
because her relationship isn't working out.

I bash its sides but nothing happens,
except my palms begin to tingle,
it simply goes on fuzzing, lost

to an electrical coma, and I know it has
retreated to that other world,
a place beyond music or meaning.

And it is only Wednesday.

Snug

I can't keep awake these days. As soon as I get home I'm underneath
the eiderdown, dozing in my tights, the radio announcer shrinking to an insect

buzzing with the news of war. If only I could let the politicians into bed
with me they might be pacified, inhale my unwashed pillowslip and milky breath

close their eyes against the amber stencil of the window frame. The Foreign
Secretary could form a spoon and tuck his knees into the opposition's flank,

Mr. President relax his grip and rest a hand there on a Middle Eastern hip.
Together we might chat in whispers of our days, interpreters translating softly

into open ears: that conference in Karachi that went on and on, crisis talks
in Belfast and New York. I'll tell of how in Norwich I unclogged the photocopier

again, sipped instant coffee, heavy-lidded in the lull of three o'clock. The Premier
of Holland will recount an anecdote in perfect English (the astounding fart

that punctured talks on agricultural policy). Eventually our giggling will stutter
to its end, our ribs relax, we'll fall into the rhythm of each other's breath

and stay like that for twelve hours at a stretch, arms around each other's middles,
dreaming not of anything we want because we have it, all there is to have.

Dictation

Furthermore, there are occasions when
I wish to raise the windowsill
and shout obscenities into the street,
loudly and with violence.
Of course I never do. *Full stop.*
Instead I offer my mistakes to be plucked out
like silver hairs by Mr. Collinson,
a small god dressed in loafers
and a double-breasted suit
who lodges in my ear all afternoon
dictating minutes of The Management Review.
But I would sooner tell you

how the sky sheds drizzle, sheer as iron filings
on a group of children shambling from school;
how I weep inside the porcelain confessionals
admitting my desire to wound, and grievously,
the hairsprayed middle manager;
how I hope to find my guardian angel
crouched inside the stationery cupboard
counting paperclips, ready to unfold
her giant wings and fly me
past the awkward fellowship of office drinks,
past desks made homely with a snapshot of the kids,
beyond the Seventh Floor executives
resplendent in their offices like cardinals,
up through stratospheres of city smog,
up into space – the boundless silence
where she'll let me go –
a million memos floating free,
the telephones of earth a distant memory.

Winter Morning

Rain sings spirituals across the pane
as Old Man River rises, rouses me
to dip a toe into the semi-dark
where half-read novels and a bowl
of last night's cereal still float.
Birds gang up in dripping trees,
already morning fills my IN tray
and I'm fantasising of the journey home.

Winter, how I love you for you speed
the darkness back to me, return me to my bed
where my titanic longings are revived
and sail around again colossally in dreams.
My bed, still almost warm, safe
as a lover whom I do not have to please.

Against Melancholy

Pick up your mat and walk!
I speak to you who ponder
on the hoar frost turning leaves
to veiny paper hearts,

you who choose to sit
in churches, votive candles
guttering to pools of wax;
I've sat there too

a few rows back,
putting questions to the gloom,
I've seen you sobbing
for the things you miss:

resist. Don't seek out
bony trees plinked silvery with rain,
look with your other eyes,
the ones you use in dreams

to see the risen dead
walk cheerfully through corridors,
testing doors, still curious
for new exquisite rooms.

A Joy Forever

I'm offering the down of my lip to a girl
who smells of purple hyacinths.
She's seen so much inside this cubicle,

legs crazed with veins, devastated thighs,
pale nipples flowering with hair;
she's heard a thousand women giving up their sighs

of supplication to their mothers, Venus,
Freya, Lakshmi, all the other minor goddesses
who gaze from magazines to show us

what we might become, if only we'd take care.
I'm also thinking of another woman
I've seen feeding pigeons in the square,

dressed in jumble, whiskers popping from her chin
like tiny wiry fireworks. Imagine letting
yourself go like that – no, imagine

yourself letting go like that, no sense of loss
for who you were, library books
cracked open in your lap while pushchairs pass

and girls with pocket mirrors hold them to the light.

Sunday at the Skin Launderette

The weekly visit to the perfumed steam. Outside
rain falls biblically, a reminder of the duty to be clean.
Inside no one notices; they're too busy with the work
of choosing a machine, counting change and making
sure the temperature's just right, trying not to pour
the powder anywhere but in the slot. Other skin

begins revolving through the plastic portholes. Skin
of fine Thai origin, Kenyan and Jamaican skin beside
the bluish white, the tattooed, mottled and poor
stretch-marked stuff, every kind of hair licked clean.
A fat man doubles over on a bench, he's making
heavy weather of it, separating folds, trying to work

his penis from its shell. It's slow and careful work.
His lungs balloon as he unsheaths his foreskin,
fragile as sushi, then the balls, until he's making
progress, loosening his mass of satin arse. Beside
him a girl unpeels her arm, a glove which comes clean
off revealing sinews. The man squeezes his paw,

fatty and raw, gathers his acreage while the girl pours
a gloss of layers over her hips, pausing to work
around the knees, the difficult toes. The clean
fug of detergents is dizzying as she drapes her skin
over her arm like an evening gown. Beside
her an old woman undresses patiently, making

sure not to tear her cobweb elbows, making
sure the birth mark is preserved. She pauses
at her clavicle and strokes the scar on the side
of her brow, puckered like a wonky zip. She works
at this delicate undoing, unpeeling the skin
which is sheer as moth wing now, until her lean

frame hangs with crushed silk, the body coming clean
at last. So they sit waiting, staring into space, making
lists in their heads, watching the machines. While his skin
tumbles dry, the man examines his heart. The women pore
over their bodies, or carefully lift their breasts to work
out once again where their souls are hiding. Outside

a skin of rain ripples the darkening streets as water pours
through gutters, pounding pavements clean, making
everything a sort of new, while the work goes on inside.

Eyelids

And finally he sculpted
these neat awnings, set them

seamlessly below the brow,
ensured they finished flush,

brushed each with lashes
to keep out disturbing drifts

of dust. His own eyes have
no covering, he chooses not

to black us out, instead remains
unblinking at the birth and

death of light, refusing
to lay down his head,

slip into other heavens,
blind to what we dream about.

The Woman who Worries Herself to Death

She wasn't robbed or raped or made a scapegoat of,
she didn't take ill-fated flights on shaky planes and

no one splashed her house in paint. Kids with hoods
and sovereign rings and hates left her alone. That twinge

she sometimes felt was just a twinge. Her fillings didn't
leak. At office do's she danced and no one laughed.

Her children didn't have disorders, fail exams,
take smack. Her husband didn't love his secretary

or get the sack. But, if you saw her fidgeting
towards the dawn, her breathing playing tricks,

a thousand *what if's* snaking in a queue, you'd feel for her,
you'd wish she had something to pin her torment to.

Modern Pastoral

The sky is red, the shepherds dream
of buxom milkmaids churning cream
while kiddies wearing caps and hoods
are setting fire to the woods.

Swigging cans of stolen beer
they know no laws, they know no fear,
sick of school they'd rather learn
how long it takes for stuff to burn.

Dictionaries and maps are good
and bibles flare like tinder wood,
and social workers' case reports
and leader articles, the thoughts

of academics with awards,
and speeches to the House of Lords,
they all go up in yellow flames
while judges with preposterous names

turn over in four-poster beds,
turn over in their learned heads
how best to deal with rising crime,
remembering another time

when neighbours left their doors ajar
and no one stole an unlocked car.
So peacefully the shepherds sleep
not knowing that their restless sheep

have wandered out through broken gates
with hooves as bright as dinner plates
and soon enough will come to learn
how long it takes for stuff to burn.

News

Tell me who is shouting these days at the tube
and if the same girl sulks at you in Woolworths

when she's handing back the change.
Taste the pennies sweating oxide in your fist.

Describe what women wear; all mismatched vests
and sandals pulled out for another year.

Record the colour of the crates where touts in shorts
sit flogging Chinese fans or fake Chanel,

pick up their fallen patter, seal it carefully with slices
of bruised strawberry.

Don't tell me about flatmates or weekends, look up
and write with accuracy of the sky.

Remind me how the night bus lurches when you're drunk,
the top deck windows grazing trees,

step out into the street – send me London, gutter-sweet
and overflowing like the bins.

Taxi Drivers

They lean against the glossy buttocks of their cabs,
kicking free of clutch and brake,

stubble-headed, right arm browner than the left,
legs whitely shocking in their shorts,

their talk, impossible to tell when distance
seals their opinions off like glass.

Five cabs ahead, the leader takes a fare, shifts
into second gear, sweeps

out of the terminal and into startling sun.
Meanwhile they wait,

June sparkling on the river's filth a mile away,
the city folded tightly in their heads.

Rodin's Lovers Interrupt their Kiss

I slid my hand from her marble thigh, removed my tongue
from her mouth and opening my eyes found someone

leaning close enough to brush us with his lips. Stepping down,
I circled him. My love drew back her hair to press an ear

against his heart. We turned our heads, saw other scattered
strangers dotting space. Hand in hand we crossed the polished floor

to study them; the grave-eyed loners, slope-armed lovers,
crocodiles of children charmed to statues in school uniform.

I touched a face in flower beneath a canvas sun. Beyond the door
another world revolved through segments made of glass.

Traffic streaked and stopped in front of watercolour lights, which
blurred from red to green then back again. A ribbon of brown river

wound away. Her fingers fell from mine so gently I could hardly
feel their absence afterwards.

Tate Modern

This is the room I return to
pacing and staring
while you are next door
watching the video
of the man
beating himself up.

Cracked roller sponge.
Abattoir light.
Cup of cold coffee,
milk skin gathered to
the star of Bethlehem.

The stepladder
is beautiful,
cordoned to keep trespassers
from climbing through the skylight,
and a shelf bears nothing
but seven silver screws
scattered like earrings.

Ladder unscalable,
screws unwearable,
cup abandoned –
oh my life!
This is the room I return to,
the room you finally tell me
is out of use
and not a piece of art.

Recycling, April

That rusty fridge has gone, one night outdoors
and now it's vanished with the sun-bleached
prints of Rome, the wonky plywood drawers
no self-respecting Oxfam would've touched.
I've claimed a tired office chair, dragged it
from its square of light into the shadows
of my flat where, like a thrifty queen, I sit.
There's something deep in all of us that knows
the joy of making good. So come with me,
we'll wait until a passer by gives pause,
extends a hand, takes in our flaws but sees
there's beauty left of sorts and so restores
us to new life. The dustbins are in bloom.
Someone will come, someone will come and soon.

Suburban Love Song

(for Lisa)

I am giving my heart to the cul-de-sac,
the loll-de-sac, the mull-de-sac,
I am falling in love
with the privacy of sodium and hedge.

Give me no prairies starved of corner shops,
no cathedrals made of history,
oceans showing off outside the door;
this is my joy, the dull-de-sac, the null-de-sac.

Once, in a ground floor flat,
I was startled from sleep by gunfire,
a woman screaming, the wail of the police;
and I wailed too, but only for myself

(this was the city after all)
I wailed for something old in me,
for something nearly lost,
a clattered gate, then silence absolute,

the beauty of a shed consuming winter light,
houses strung together in a loop;
the sigh-de-sac, the lull-de-sac,
mysterious and mundane as a kiss.

What Not to Do with Your Day

Don't make another trip to the municipal library
where you try to avoid the overweight librarian
who's spotted you one too many times already and probably
has you in a box marked 'Regular'
along with the man who trails a Tesco's carrier bag
and gabbles to the computer instructing it to
beam him up.
Don't brush your hand along the shelves, depressed
by all the works of genius you'll never read
then meander home through unconvincing sunlight
turning over the same old thoughts.
At home, don't spend three-quarters of an hour at the piano
trying to master *Leaving on a Jet Plane.*
Don't return in half an hour's time for another shot.
Don't scoff three chocolate mini rolls and then feel slightly sick
or decide a cup of coffee will
'perk you up' then worry the caffeine
is staining your teeth.
Don't turn the examination of your teeth into
a search for errant facial hair
and reason that, since you're not going anywhere,
now is the time to deal with the problem.
If you have a television set, don't switch it on.
Don't watch an interview
with a personality unknown to you,
don't bother with the kids' TV show either, the one presented by
a suntanned girl who talks at you in a shouty voice.
Don't hate her for a long time afterwards for being banal
and well paid. And as the light finally gives up, leaving you
to contemplate a pile of newspapers from last weekend,
don't decide to have a go at *Leaving on a Jet Plane*
one last time.

Experimental Concert

When I arrive late and the sound of my anorak crackling is louder than the music, I know I've made a terrible mistake. *Open your mind,* my good self whispers. But Oh God, Oh God, there's a man suppressing the valves of a saxophone so when he blows nothing comes out, except maybe a little spittle. His accompanist is at a laptop engineering every now and then a gentle plinky plonk. The saxophonist gets out the sort of sponge you scour dishes with and rubs the green side very gently on the mouthpiece of his instrument, slowly near the microphone. We stare. He rubs and wipes, rubs and wipes. Once, I met a woman who told me she was writing a thesis on gender politics in Cagney and Lacey, and I laughed saying that was a good one. She looked confused. I wished I were somewhere else. But not here: no one could wish that hard. The plinking goes on and in my heart I'm wishing Ken Dodd would sing *Happiness,* I'm in love with Max Bygraves waving his big bland hands, I'm willing to *Tie a Yellow Ribbon, Save the Last Waltz, Cry for Argentina,* if only it would stop. And when at last it does, and we've clapped like hostages presented with blue sky, I leave, my anorak performing encores to the night.

Charity Shop

Here are the kaftans and the ski-pants of our youth,
those suits that never suited us, this is where our seasons meet,

a fur, a swimming costume flung off on a vanished beach.
The air hangs with a perfume bottled long ago,

a scent worn by the mannequin got up like Mother of the Bride,
while zipped in cellophane a wedding dress stays fresh.

The few who've come to shop here move as visitors
in someone else's home, picking up and setting down the ornaments –

the ashtray printed with a portrait of the Queen,
the maiden made in China flourishing her parasol. Now and then

an elderly assistant brings another item to the light –
an orphaned milk jug, or a small cack-handed painting of the sea,

and someone knows they've waited all their life to find it there
among the yellow paperbacks, the cardboard box of scratched LPs.

Riverton Rocks, 1959

I came across the photograph by accident,
a scrap of black and white, the date and place
washed pale: a woman on a picnic rug,
her dress frothed out around her like a wave.
The young man at her side is smiling, though
uncertainly, as if responding to a joke he can't
quite understand, his blond quiff tips
off balance in the wind. She wears his ring.

It's late on in the afternoon, long shadows fall
across her legs, and in this light, her calves
and feet resemble mine. Whoever holds the camera
counts, and her fiancé pulls her nearer with both arms
as if he knows that when the shutter clucks she'll break

politely from the circle he has made for her
and look out far beyond the rocks, to cameras poised
on rainy English beaches, and another man – my father,
standing on the shingle, cradling an empty space.

Six Months

(for Eva Sharkey)

What you know, are the only things worth knowing,
you, who give yourself whole
into the arms of strangers,

unafraid of meeting their eyes.
You who ponder your findings,
serene as a pope on your blue changing mat.

Teach us not to care about causing a fuss,
teach us to eat when we're hungry,
to be ambivalent to fashion, to bear no grudges,

and to love without restraint
this yellow leaf, this face, this universe
composed of passing colours, temporary shapes.

The Concert Pianist's Mother

I've been knitting you a scarf, looping
wool around my forefinger,
pulling it into a stitch.
Royal blue, like the tie you wore
for your first competition
in that town hall fifteen miles from home.
Sometimes, when I'm washing up,
I hear your last note singing like a spoon
against a glass and see you

opening your eyes to find your own hands
lifting from the keys, the way I lift
my fingers from the suds
and spread them out in front of me.
Amazing. Mine.

Angels at Rest

Through the bracken and the overgrowth they come,
huge iridescent sandaled feet,

hoisting each other up, then sprawling in the trees
like celestial tigers. They detect

aspirins crunched like ginger-nuts in nearby towns,
but stay put, tired of hovering

at bedsides (the wallpapers ever in bloom), tired
of collecting where cars collide,

preferring this, the graveyard's mustard light, the gnats,
late summer turning over with the dead.

It doesn't last, of course. A woman picks through grass,
bluebells wilting in her fist, finds a stone

and bends, begins to cry. The angels sigh,
sad for the smallness of the living,

the living, with their expansive novels and their bluebells,
their millions of ideas and manifestos,

their billion worries too (free falling aircraft, armies of irate
diseases) more real to them than flame-

lit trees. The angels beat their wings and contemplate
the gnats instead, specks

of almost nothing, massed like clouds, their un-seeing eyes,
their fathomless, microscopic hearts.

Awake in the Far Away

I like it here: it's easier to scan the internet
for news of hurricanes
or read the rules of wrestling, or look up recipes
for Won Ton Soup.
They let me decorate the Post-It notes with rhymes
and stick them to reports until they're frilly
as Flamenco dancers' skirts. Olé!
There are orchids in reception.
No one writes their names on biscuit tins.

I like the boss who blushes easily and can't avoid
that luscious girl in marketing although
he tries (I've seen him pick up telephones
with no one on the other end).
I like the fug of heaters turned up full,
the clouds blown sideways
while I type *Dear Sir,*
the buses as they crawl like rainy ladybirds
down Prince of Wales Road.
And no one asks me what
I'm doing here, or if I'll stay, they simply
smile and make their way along the corridors.

There was a time before this empty board room,
I am sure, a time before this chart
flipped clean,
although it must be further off than childhood.
It's three o'clock and May;
I stand still with the tray of cups
and watch a cyclist unlock his bike.
Somewhere a telephone begins to ring.

Handbag Thief

Alone at last and you're unpacking everything:
the broken-spoked umbrella,
Plumbstruck lipstick, thriller
destined for a bin on Oxford Street.

Ignoring tissues and the half-popped
packet of Ibuprofen, which crackles
like lit tinder at your touch,
you seize the purse, transfer the twenties

cash point clean into the warm
back pocket of your jeans,
but leave the pennies and receipts,
the number of a man I met last week.

My telephone is ready for your speech,
befriend my friends or listen
to my voice apologise for failing
to pick up. The compact camera

fits your palm, you grin and turn
the last exposure on yourself,
a flash of teeth and bed-sit wallpaper.
We're floating in a dark room

side-by-side, my tan preserved between
your fingertips. Only when it seems
there's nothing left, unzip the inside
pocket and remove the poem scribbled

on an envelope: raise it like an X-ray
to the light. I'll leave you there
to finish it, chewing on my ballpoint,
drawing on my final cigarette.

On the Day that You were Born

The angels got together and decided to create
a dream come true.
Sorry, no, that wasn't you.
On the day that you were born
it rained incessantly.
Three potholers were carried to their deaths
by flashfloods in North Wales.
In Manchester a man came home
and set about his wife
with woodwork tools.
Everywhere the sky was dark by four o'clock.
There might have been an air disaster too –
in fact there was,
two hundred people dropped into a field.
No one survived.

Stationery

Your love of it will get you into trouble one day:
another pristine biro sliding from the box –
two midnight blue, one red for danger, red
for stop – the extra notebook lifted from a pile
pressed clean as hotel sheets. Everyone is somewhere
else, they're spooning Nescafé into their favourite
mugs, watching clouds dissolve like screensavers.

Quickly, palm a roll of Sellotape, a pastel block
of Post-It notes. Award yourself a staple gun
for all that unpaid overtime (the city shrinking
to a nest of lights, your own reflection watching
itself reconciling columns of accounts). Choose
scissors with expensive blades; paperclips
to fasten loose-leaf days; a jumbo marker fat enough

for making signs that could be read from planes.
Close your eyes, inhale the dizzy dark of chemicals,
allow yourself a moment more before you turn
back to the corridor, back towards the cricked neck
of your Anglepoise spotlighting everything
that's still undone. Leave the boxes of buff envelopes
untouched – some with windows, some without.

Learning to Spell

Sometimes, on sopping autumn afternoons
I see Miss Ferris rising from her desk
to chalk in sloping script across the board:
dissatisfied, accommodate, successfully,
words we should use correctly in our lives.

Because I failed her tests so miserably
she led me up the staircase to her room
where exercise books balanced on the table
near a filmy cup of coffee she hadn't
time to drink, and on the easy chair

Far From the Madding Crowd splayed open
like a fallen bird. Miss Ferris looked at me,
"It's wonderful," she said, with her embarrassed
smile, then turned away and hunted out
the spelling book that still sits on my shelf,

unread. That year I tried the novel
for myself, and found Miss Ferris offering
her fine unpowdered face to Gabriel Oak.
They kissed, her arms encircled him, while on
her breast her crucifix lay shivering.

Shoestring Dialogues

and on and on they talked, en route to the cemetery
and the giant multiplex (half price on Tuesday),

past the cowsheds where the cows were being
avant-garde and milky, saying this and that, or singing.

Theirs was not terrific talk, not Oscar Wilde stuff
but still, they had ideas, philosophies, they had enough,

more than enough to laugh about; they liked to laugh,
they did it everywhere, except the library (the staff

would shoot them dirty looks although their fun
was clean). They rode their conversation on the 41,

flung it head first in a swimming pool. *No Petting*
said the sign. They made up others – *No Forgetting,*

No Fretting, No Getting Wet-ing. With the taste
of chlorine in their throats, they dressed,

recounting stories of when this, when that, when
something else, still talking they walked out of town

towards his flat – lean, like him and down at heel.
They settled on the sofa. Dusk arrived. Meanwhile

a shoal of silverfish woke up the bathroom
turning it to dazzle, hazardous, and pretty soon

the lights about the neighbourhood came on.
He made her pumpkin soup. She ate a crouton

and he watched her crunch; she wasn't like his other
loves, her face was round and freckled, neither

was she shy, like them, but smiled openly. Her hands
were small and quick to paint the air with sounds,

she was her own conductor and he told her so.
They spoke more quietly of people they'd once known,

entering the locked rooms in each other's heads,
picking up the traces of each other's dead. She made

a place inside his arms. The clock struck three.
They closed their eyes, consulted and agreed.

Afternoon Song

It is nice in the asylum – it smells of peaches all day long. Better here, with the soft edges of the board games, than out in the rain that never calls you by your Christian name. Here there are lights-out by eleven and Cup-a-Soups which you can help yourself to any time you please. There are no characters in clogs or white starched overalls – it's not that kind of outfit – instead there is Mike who keeps a note in loopy hand-writing of 'how you're getting on' and you know that if you asked to take a look, he'd turn over the file and say "See, nothing to hide" showing you his palms. There are no secrets here, even during sleep, we tell each other everything – Philip's mother chasing spoons through corridors, Meg's old boyfriend dressed as Mary Queen of Scots. Tomorrow we're expecting the begonias to blossom, en masse or individually, pink or orange or navy blue: one of them, at least, is bound to open soon.

Going to the Dogs with Mickey Rooney

Now, at eighty-something years he's shrunk to less
than five foot three, which causes some difficulty

because the crowd is dense and loud, and instead
of struggling for a view he wants to start on about

how Laurence Olivier once called him the best actor
in Hollywood, and did I know that when he first

appeared on stage he was seventeen months old,
wowing the audience by tooting a tiny mouth-organ?

He's just not getting this, I think to myself,
I haven't come to Walthamstow to hear about

Our Gang or *Babes on Broadway* – so I pass him
my binoculars, and steer him in the direction

of the bunny, a white flash streaking the track,
the lashing greyhounds in their numbered vests,

tongues lolling pink, coats glossy in the floodlight
as fresh paint. "I've got sixty quid on Assistant

Producer," I shout. And Mickey all at once
is clambering onto the bench, waving his arms, crying

"Move, you sonovabitch" like the Brooklyn Joe
he used to be until his mother changed his name

in 1926. Afterwards we'll get a pie and peas,
discuss his wives; perhaps I'll let him play-punch me.

Agoraphobic in Love

The world he leads me to is written in Chinese,
I am its foreigner. Pushchairs, pigeons, effluent,
dogs going off their heads and everywhere queues
of people breathing. Workmen in fluorescent
jackets hammer tarmac. Buses get too close.
The crescent moons rise purple in my palms,
and though I want to be airlifted home, I choose
to have my heart attack with him, his arms
around my waist. He pulls me through collapsing
corridors of light (my God, through market stalls)
but even as we're chatting I am busy practicing
a thousand mantras in my head, *let me not fail*
at this, let me not fail. His fingernails are neatly
trimmed, his smile lazy. Could I need him more
than walls? More than pills? More than my keys?
Could I depend on him like Amazon, might our
shared future include aeroplanes?

                              Now he brings
me to this coastal town, we sit on shingle staring
as the waves repeat themselves. A seagull flings
itself into a baking sheet of sky and terrifying
children pass, dribbling ice-cream. My hands
are folded into his. I sip the air. The past
is bolted up and locked away. As daylight ends
I'm praying this will last, praying I can *make* it last.

Almonds

My wife says hardship feeds the soul.
Sometimes I prize my belly more.
I think of how she's hobbled on her knees
up raw stone steps. She's made the pilgrimage
to Santiago de Compostela, and each Good Friday
joins the faithful shouldering their solemn way
behind the cross. At three o'clock she's prostrate,
faint with fasting and the heat. I've told her
she's too old to treat herself so harshly, but her soul
has such an appetite. I'm not as strong.
This afternoon I called into the church
to say a prayer before Saint James,
but minutes later and my mind was feasting
on the flesh of nectarines, plucking
mussels from their shells. I blessed myself and rose.
The street was white and empty
when I pushed my way into the sun.
Siesta, and the wealthy lunching in cool restaurants;
langoustine, perhaps a glass or two of musky
red to complement a plate of quails served
with tender vegetables. The slice of spoons
through silken custard caramels.
At home I rested on my chair, poured out
my rosary, a chain of chickpeas, on the table top
and opening the cupboard door discovered
there had been no miracle. Everything
was as before; the cured ham, cheap and tough,
a staling loaf, and there the dish of almonds
smooth and sharp as flints. I didn't curse.
Instead I found the mortar, took a handful
of the almonds and began to grind,
crushing every small hard heart against the stone.
I cut a slab of butter, mashed the almonds in,
then added pepper, salt, a squeeze
of lemon juice. Later I would spread the mixture thickly
on a slice of bread. My wife would smile. I climbed upstairs
and lay down in our shuttered room, sustained.

Sarah Masterson in Middle Age

Marry the man today and change his ways tomorrow.
                    – (Guys and Dolls)

Long before Bacardis in Havana
and the tipsy schoolgirl act, I knew;
his suits, his casual wedge of fifty
dollar bills. His sad saint eyes.
The way he'd tip his hat at loss
then roll towards the next big win.
My sky. I free-fell into him.
And it was Paradise created
fresh in New York City every day.

Sometimes he'd disappear for three
nights at a time, then come in
early morning glowing and unshaven.
Flush. I'd pour us coffee, scold,
then await his sure apology –
a whirl around the night-clubs
pink with dancing girls (although
he only danced with me). Until
the music faded out. Until he didn't

call home late and promise me
a rainbow wrapped in cellophane,
but started substituting *Dear* for *Doll*.
One afternoon, I found his marker
tucked inside The Book of Deutoronomy.
Listened, speechless over dinner when
he said he'd cashed his chips and what
about that little house in Maine?
Tonight he wears the crewneck

that I knitted years ago for fun.
I think of how he swung me round
and flopped me on our bed, sunlight
turning us to angels on the quilt.
I look at him, my Obadiah, paging
through *The Racing Record,* just
for old-times' sake. His dice redundant
on the shelf. My uniform dull-buttoned,
hanging in the closet out of sight.

Afterword

I also lied about the therapy; I lay back on a bench instead and told my troubles to a drunk who stank of stale cider and relieved me of my cigarettes. I lied about my one good kidney and the ballet lessons. And the pills. I lied about my childhood in Somerset where I learned the taste of crab apples and swam like Esther Williams in a turquoise lake wearing a costume splashed with orange sunflowers. The Yew tree is still waiting to grow in the garden I never knew. I have always believed in God and I do not speak Portuguese. Cape Cod is a mystery to me. You might be wondering about the man with whom I waited outside the tobacconist until the rain eased off. But that's all beside the point and too late now. There are other things we ought to get cleared up: I never got beyond the shaving scene in *Ulysses*. It was me who took the wheels off your car. Your shoulders really are lopsided.

The Road to Persia

There was a twinkle of tummy where your shirt poked open.
I put the pad of my finger on the space
and it matched exactly. This embarrassed you a little
and I was sorry I'd made you feel uncomfortable.
You ordered the grape chicken and I the lamb cutlets
which arrived dressed in a mysterious green sauce.
The music reminded me of the bizarre opera singing
in *The Fifth Element* and we agreed we didn't like that film.
There were three types of rice – orange, plain and dill.
You said something funny, I don't remember what,
and we'd swapped places, so you were sitting by the draft
and I was wondering if you might be cold, even though
you're basically a human radiator, you go about in your shirtsleeves
when other people are wearing coats.
Neither of us had any intention of making declarations,
not when I had some kind of sniffle
and hadn't washed my hair, and you were generally exhausted
after some meeting, so neither of us knew afterwards exactly how it happened,
how one moment we were eating rice and talking about *The Fifth Element,*
and the next you were leaning over the table to kiss me
while the staff cleared tables.
So, all I'm saying is I'm glad there will be other things to laugh about
and types of rice we haven't tasted yet, and films that neither of us will enjoy.